High Integrity Software

The SPARK Approach to Safety and Security

Sample Chapters

High Integrity Software

The SPARK Approach to Safety and Security

JOHN BARNES

with Praxis Critical Systems Limited

 ADDISON-WESLEY

An imprint of Pearson Education

London • Boston • Indianapolis • New York • Mexico City
Toronto • Sydney • Tokyo • Singapore • Hong Kong • Cape Town
New Delhi • Madrid • Paris • Amsterdam • Munich • Milan

PEARSON EDUCATION LIMITED

Head Office:
Edinburgh Gate
Harlow CM20 2JE
Tel: +44 (0) 1279 623623
Fax: +44 (0) 1279 431059

London Office:
128 Long Acre
London WC2E 9AN
Tel: +44 (0) 207 447 2000
Fax: +44 (0) 207 447 2170

Website: *www.awprofessional.com*

First printed in Great Britain in 2003.

© 2003 Praxis Critical Systems Limited.

The right of John Barnes to be identified as author of this Work has been asserted by him in accordance with the Copyright, Designs and Patents Act 1988.

ISBN 0-321-19973-1

Typeset by John Barnes Informatics
Printed and bound in Great Britain by **Ashford Colour Press, Gosport, Hampshire.**

The Publisher's policy is to use paper manufactured from sustainable forests.

*There are two ways of constructing a software design. One way is to make it so simple that there are **obviously** no deficiencies. And the other way is to make it so complicated that there are no **obvious** deficiencies.*

Professor C. A. R. Hoare
The 1980 Turing award lecture

Foreword

To the participants, the early years of SPARK were more than just exciting...
The first challenge was to produce, rather rapidly, a formally-based
computational model and analysis tools, for a core of Ada large enough to be
considered a usable language. At the time, even compilation of Ada was still
regarded as a major undertaking, and few people believed rigorous static-
analysis methods could ever 'scale up' to industrial proportions; bringing the
two together was seen as a rather wild enterprise. The idea was nevertheless
brought to fruition, through the imaginative talent and determination of the
youthful SPARK team at PVL (Program Validation Limited) that I was so
privileged to lead at that time. There were too many of them to name here, but
a number of their works are cited in the Bibliography. The success of this first
phase of the development of SPARK also owed much to the confidence and
sympathetic help of the early users of SPARK, guiding us in the right direction.

SPARK is more than a programming language – it is a way of conceiving
programs. To use it to advantage, in concert with one's other preferred
software development paradigms, requires a very good understanding of what
it offers. The second important phase in the development of SPARK – this time
as a support for the software design and development process – required direct
involvement in high integrity Ada projects on a much larger scale than PVL
could undertake. Crucial to this was the vision of Praxis Critical Systems (in
which PVL is now incorporated), in recognizing the potential of the
technology, and fielding it judiciously in large projects to great advantage. It
has been pleasing to see the change in SPARK users' perception of software
verification, from a retrospectively-applied purgative, inflicting on the
developer a level of pain matching the integrity level required – to an integral
part of a software development process aimed at getting it right first time. It
should not really be surprising that techniques that help to produce the right
product can also be economically beneficial; and indeed, our gradual absorption
into a cultural movement towards Correctness by Construction has been very
good news.

It is said that most of the best books never get written. For some time we
had agonized over the need to inform the wider programming community of

what SPARK can accomplish; although there were many successful applications, it remained very difficult to discover enough about SPARK to use it well. Yet it seemed that a good exposition of the subject would remain a dream forever. What a joy and a relief that John Barnes, having developed an interest in SPARK over a number of years, and having experienced the need for a book, should write it for us! And better, so much better, than we could have done ourselves!

Obviously John shares our belief in the importance of language, in shaping and implementing one's ideas in software. But his healthy scepticism of the usefulness of formalization, his energetic questioning of every aspect of SPARK, took us on a new voyage of discovery, casting an interesting new light on the language. And when it came to the adaptation to Ada 95 (on which John is an expert, being the principal author of the official Ada 95 Rationale), the decisions on how SPARK should be extended at this time were rather obvious to him.

The reader will enjoy John Barnes' lively guidance through SPARK. With panache, he combines rigorous clarity and a great sense of fun.

Bernard Carré
Southampton, England
April 1997

As a now less-youthful member of Bernard Carré's 'youthful SPARK team' at Program Validation Limited, I find it satisfying to see how SPARK has matured. With that growing maturity, it has also become much more widely accepted, thanks in a large part to earlier editions of this book. Many of the trends observed by Bernard in his 1997 Foreword have developed an increased momentum and some new ones have become discernible.

The migration of static analysis from a painful, post-hoc verification exercise to an integral part of a sound development process is now well-established. Users who have espoused 'correctness by construction' and allowed the design-by-contract™ facilities of SPARK to strengthen their designs have been rewarded with improved quality, lower defect rates and reduced cost (a result that should not surprise any professional engineer).

Progressive refinement of SPARK, together with the rapid increase in computing horsepower provided by current hardware, has also made it easier to apply in the harsh reality of the industrial 'real world'. In particular, proof of exception freedom is now a wholly practical exercise for any high integrity system; a result of particular interest to the security community for whom 'buffer overflow' attacks remain a serious problem.

The sustained success of SPARK can be traced to its sound logical and mathematical underpinnings. SPARK is good engineering and good engineering endures as fashions change.

Peter Amey
Bath, England
December 2002

Preface

This book is about programming in SPARK – a language highly suited for writing programs that need to be reliable, and thus particularly relevant to those application areas where safety or security are important. It is a major revision of the previous book which was entitled *High Integrity Ada*.

SPARK is sometimes regarded as being just a subset of Ada with various annotations that you have to write as Ada comments. This is mechanically correct but is not at all the proper view to take. SPARK should be seen as a distinct language in its own right and that is one reason why the title was changed in this edition.

SPARK has just those features required for writing reliable software: not so austere as to be a pain, but not so rich as to make program analysis out of the question. But it is sensible to share compiler technology with some other standard language and it so happens that Ada provides a better framework than many other languages. In fact, Ada seems to be the only language that has good lexical support for the concept of programming by contract by separating the ability to describe a software interface (the contract) from its implementation (the code) and enabling these to be analysed and compiled separately. The Eiffel language has created a strong interest in the concept of programming by contract which SPARK has embodied since its inception in the late 1980s.

There has recently also been interest in reliable software in areas other than those that have traditionally cared about reliability (avionics and railroads). It is now beginning to be realized that reliable software matters in other areas, such as finance, communications, medicine and motor cars.

Accordingly, I have changed the presentation with the goal that no knowledge of Ada is required to understand the discussion. However, there are some remarks comparing SPARK and Ada which will be helpful to those who do know Ada. Most of these are confined to the ends of sections and are in a different font but just a few are embedded in the text in square brackets. Either way they should not impede the discussion for the general reader.

I have always been interested in techniques for writing reliable software, if only (presumably like most programmers) because I would like my programs to work without spending ages debugging the wretched things.

Perhaps my first realization that the tools used really mattered came with my experience of using Algol 60 when I was a programmer in the chemical industry. It was a delight to use a compiler that stopped me violating the bounds of arrays; it seemed such an advance over Fortran and other even more primitive languages which allowed programs to violate themselves in an arbitrary manner.

On the other hand I have always been slightly doubtful of the practicality of the formal theorists who like to define everything in some turgid specification language before contemplating the process known as programming. It has always seemed to me that formal specifications were pretty obscure to all but a few and might perhaps even make a program less reliable in a global sense by increasing the problem of communication between client and programmer.

Nevertheless, I have often felt that underlying mathematical foundations can provide us with better tools even if the mathematical nature is somewhat hidden by a more practical façade. For example, enumeration types are really about sets but a deep understanding of set theory is not necessary in order to obtain the benefits of strong typing by realizing that a set of apples is not the same as a set of oranges.

SPARK has this flavour of practical helpfulness underpinned by solid mathematical foundations. You don't have to understand the theorems of Böhm and Jacopini in order to obtain the benefits of good flow structure. Equally, SPARK does not require esoteric annotations of a formal kind but quite simple affirmations of access and visibility which enable the SPARK Examiner to effectively 'look over your shoulder' and identify inconsistencies between what you said you were going to do in the annotations and what you actually did in the code.

One of the advantages of SPARK is that it may be used at various levels. At the simplest level of data flow analysis, the annotations ensure that problems of mistaken identity do not arise, that undefined values are not used and other similar flow errors are trapped. The next level of information flow analysis gives additional assurance regarding the inter-dependence between variables and can highlight unexpected relationships indicative of poorly organized data.

For certain applications, formal proof may be useful and SPARK provides a third level in which formal preconditions, postconditions and other assertions enable proofs to be established with the aid of the SPARK tools.

However, formal proof is easily oversold; the effort involved in developing a proof can be high and in many cases might well be spent more effectively on other aspects of ensuring that a program is fit for its purpose. So the ability to apply SPARK at various levels according to the application is extremely valuable.

A simple use of proof is in showing that a program is free from exceptions due to run-time errors such as those caused by overflow or writing outside an array. This can be done in a straightforward manner and does not require the addition of the more detailed annotations required for proof in general.

The various levels of analysis might even be mixed in a single program. The fine detail of key algorithms might be formally proved, higher organizational parts might benefit from information flow analysis, whereas the overall driving routines could well need only data flow analysis. And proof of freedom from run-time errors might be applied to the whole program.

I must say a little about the background to this book. I first encountered the foundation work done by Bob Phillips at Malvern when a consultant to the British Government and tasked with monitoring the usefulness of various research activities. I remember feeling that the flow analysis he was investigating was potentially good stuff but needed practical user interfaces.

That was twenty-five years ago. The current language and tools reflect the enormous energy put into the topic since then by Bernard Carré and his colleagues, first at Southampton University, then at Program Validation Limited and later at Praxis Critical Systems. The original approach was for the analysis of existing programs but now the emphasis is much more on writing the programs correctly in the first place.

However, it always seemed to me that although the tools and techniques were gaining steady acceptance, nevertheless both the tools and indeed the world of programmers deserved a more accessible description than that found in conference papers and user manuals.

A big impetus to actually do something was when my daughter Janet and I were invited by Program Validation Limited to join in a review of the formal definition of SPARK and its further development. This resulted in a report familiarly known as *Janet and John go a-Sparking* (non-British readers should note that there is a series of children's books concerning the activities of Janet and John). Being involved in the review strengthened my feeling that a book would be very appropriate and, thanks to the support of Praxis, led to the first version of this book in 1997.

Since then, SPARK and its tools have evolved further to include the safe parts of object oriented programming, a better means of interfacing to other parts of a system, a simpler means of showing that a program is free from exceptions, and more auditable means of proving that a program is correct. The various tools are also greatly improved both in terms of speed and quality of reporting.

These improvements justified this new book and I am most grateful for the support of Praxis in enabling me to write it. The CD at the back includes the latest demonstration versions of the major tools and electronic copies of a great deal of further documentation as well as the exercises and answers. More information regarding Praxis and SPARK will be found at www.sparkada.com.

I must now thank all those who have helped in many different ways. The external reviewers included Kung-Kiu Lau, George Romanski, Jim Sutton, Tucker Taft and Phil Thornley; their comments were extremely valuable in ensuring that the book met its main objectives. I was greatly assisted by a number of staff of Praxis Critical Systems and I am especially grateful to Peter Amey, Rod Chapman, Jonathan Hammond and Adrian Hilton for their detailed comments and encouragement.

I must also continue to thank Bernard Carré for his vision in getting it all going; Bernard has now retired to warmer climes but his good work lives on.

Finally, many thanks to my wife Barbara for her help in typesetting and proofreading, to friends at Addison-Wesley for their continued guidance and to Sheila Chatten for her help in the final stages of production.

John Barnes
Caversham, England
December 2002

Contents

Part 1

An Overview

This first part comprises three chapters which cover the background to SPARK and provide a broad overview of the main features of the language and its associated tools.

Chapter 1 starts with a brief account of the categories of software, the need for reliable software and the idea that individual pieces of software should have to satisfy contracts defining what they do. It then discusses the key requirements of a language for high integrity systems and explains how SPARK with its various annotations meets those requirements. There is then a very brief introduction to the main SPARK tools which comprise the Examiner, Simplifier and Proof Checker and this is followed by a couple of simple examples. The chapter concludes with some historical remarks regarding the origins of SPARK and the structure of the book.

Chapter 2 discusses the general principles of decomposition through abstraction and the concepts of Abstract State Machines, Type Extension and Abstract Data Types. It then illustrates the major features of the SPARK language through a number of examples of these abstractions. The chapter concludes with an introduction to the important topics of refinement and program composition. In a sense this chapter provides an overview of the second part of the book which discusses the SPARK core language in detail.

Chapter 3 introduces the main SPARK tools and the process of proof which form the topics of the third part of the book. It starts with some philosophical remarks on correctness and then introduces the use of the Examiner for flow analysis. It concludes with an outline of the use of path functions and the generation and proof of verification conditions.

1 Introduction

SPARK is a high level programming language designed for writing software for high integrity applications. In this introductory chapter we briefly outline the main objectives of SPARK, its background and the overall structure of the rest of this book.

It is perhaps difficult to give a rigid definition of high integrity applications other than to say that they are applications where it is important for the program to be well written. High integrity applications include both safety and security. Safety critical applications are usually defined to be those where life and limb or the environment are at risk if the program is in error, whereas security applications concern the integrity of information or the access to it. But clearly any application benefits from being written correctly and the merit of SPARK is that it enables errors to be prevented or detected in a more predictable manner.

1.1   Software and its problems

Software pervades all aspects of our modern society. Banking systems, transport systems, medical systems, industrial control systems and office systems all depend upon the functioning of software. As a consequence the safety of many human lives and the security of much property now depends upon the correctness of software.

Software takes many forms and there are many styles of application. At one extreme is the casual calculation on a pocket calculator or similar machine. Speed of programming and immediacy of answer are key considerations.

Then there are office programs such as spreadsheets and word processors. These highly interactive programs are the subject of much attention and market driven development. They tend not to be critical. If incorrect, a word processor may crash and lose data but disaster does not strike (except perhaps that the user may get angry and suffer a heart attack). The specification of such programs is not given; they do what they do and the user learns by experience.

And finally there are serious programs that, if incorrect, cause real difficulties. These range from safety critical programs such as engine controllers to programs in communications systems where security is a major concern. For safety critical programs the consequence of any error can be loss of life or damage to the environment. For secure programs the consequence of an error may be equally catastrophic such as loss of national security or commercial reputation or just plain theft. In addition, large programs of any kind often have their own problems resulting from complexity and these frequently lead to economic embarrassment through delays in commissioning.

Both safety critical and secure systems may be designed with great care and contain physical back up, locks and other devices; however, their ultimate integrity depends upon the correctness of the underpinning software.

What do we mean by correct software? Perhaps a general definition is software that does what the user had in mind. And 'had in mind' might literally mean just that for a simple one-off program written to do an ad-hoc calculation or, for a large avionics application, it might be interpreted as the text of some contract between the ultimate client and the software developer.

This idea of a contract is not new. If we look at the programming libraries developed in the early 1960s, particularly in mathematical areas and perhaps written in Algol 60 (a language favoured for the publication of such material in respected journals such as the *Communications of the ACM* and the *Computer Journal*), we find that the manual tells us what parameters are required, any constraints on their range and so on. In essence there is a contract between the writer of the subroutine and the user. The user promises to hand over suitable parameters and the subroutine promises to produce the correct answer.

The decomposition of a program into various component parts is very familiar and the essence of the programming process is to define what these parts do and therefore the interfaces between them. This enables the parts to be developed independently of each other. If we write each part correctly (that is so that it satisfies its side of the contract implied by its interface) and if we have defined the interfaces correctly then we are assured that when we put the parts together to create the complete system, it will work correctly.

Bitter experience shows that life is not quite like that. Two things go wrong: on the one hand the interface definitions are not usually complete (there are holes in the contracts) and on the other hand, the individual components are not correct or are used incorrectly (the contracts are violated). And of course the contracts might not say what we meant to say anyway.

It is these problems that SPARK addresses by using techniques whose overall goal is to develop correct programs with less total effort than with conventional languages.

1.2   **Correctness by construction**

SPARK encourages the development of programs in an orderly manner with the aim that the program should be correct by virtue of the techniques used in its construction. This 'correctness by construction' approach is in marked contrast to other approaches which aim to generate as much code as quickly as possible in order to have something to demonstrate.

There is strong evidence from a number of years of use of SPARK in application areas such as avionics and railway signalling [Amey, 2002] that indeed, not only is the program more likely to be correct, but the overall cost of development is actually less in total after all the testing and integration phases are taken into account.

We will now look in a little more detail at the two problem areas introduced above, first giving complete interface definitions, and secondly ensuring that the code correctly implements the interface.

Ideally, the definition of the interfaces between the software components should hide all irrelevant detail but expose all relevant detail. Alternatively we might say that an interface definition should be both complete and correct.

As a simple example of an interface definition consider the interface to a subprogram (method). As just mentioned, the interface should describe the full contract between the user and the implementor. The details of how the subprogram is implemented should not concern us. In order that these two concerns be clearly distinguished it is helpful to use a programming language in which they are lexically distinct. Unfortunately not many languages are like this. Popular languages such as Java, C and Eiffel usually present subprograms as one lump with the interface physically bound to the implementation. This is a nuisance because not only does it make checking the interface less straightforward since the compiler wants the whole code but it also encourages the developer to hack the code at the same time as writing the interface and this confuses the logic of the development process.

However, Ada has such a structure separating interface (known as a specification) from the implementation (a body). This applies both to individual subprograms (procedures or functions) and to groups of entities encapsulated into packages and this is one reason why Ada was chosen as a base for SPARK.

SPARK requires additional information to be provided and this is done through the mechanism of annotations which conveniently take the form of Ada comments. A key purpose of these annotations is to increase the amount of information about the interface without providing unnecessary information about the implementation. In fact SPARK allows the information to be added at various levels of detail as appropriate to the needs of the application.

Consider the information given by the following Ada specification

```
procedure Add(X: in Integer);
```

Frankly, it tells us very little. It just says that there is a procedure called Add and that it takes a single parameter of type Integer whose formal name is X. This is enough to enable the compiler to generate code to call the procedure. But it says nothing about what the procedure does. It might do anything at all.

It certainly doesn't have to add anything nor does it have to use the value of X. It could for example subtract two unrelated global variables and print the result to some file. But now consider what happens when we add the lowest level of SPARK annotation. The specification might become

       procedure Add(X: **in** Integer);
       --# **global in out** Total;

This states that the only global variable that the procedure can access is that called Total. Moreover the mode information tells us that the initial value of Total must be used (**in**) and that a new value will be produced (**out**). The SPARK rules also say more about the parameter X. Although in Ada a parameter need not be used at all, nevertheless an **in** parameter must be used in SPARK.

So now we know rather a lot. We know that a call of Add will produce a new value of Total and that it will use the initial value of Total and the value of X. We also know that Add cannot affect anything else. It certainly cannot print anything or have any other malevolent side effect.

Of course, the information regarding the interface is not complete since nowhere does it require that addition be performed in order to obtain the new value of Total. In order to do this we can add optional annotations which concern proof and obtain

       procedure Add(X: **in** Integer);
       --# **global in out** Total;
       --# **post** Total = Total~ + X;

The annotation commencing **post** is called a postcondition and explicitly says that the final value of Total is the result of adding its initial value (distinguished by ~) to that of X. So now the specification is complete.

It is also possible to provide preconditions. Thus we might require X to be positive and we could express this by

       --# **pre** X > 0;

As we shall see later, an important aspect of the SPARK annotations is that they are all checked statically by the SPARK Examiner and other tools and not when the program executes. These tools are outlined in Section 1.5.

It is especially important to note that the pre- and postconditions are checked before the program executes. If they were only checked when the program executes then it would be a bit like bolting the door after the horse has bolted (which reveals a nasty pun caused by overloading in English!). We don't really want to be told that the conditions are violated as the program runs. For example we might have a precondition for landing an aircraft

       procedure Touchdown(...);
       --# **pre** Undercarriage_Down;

It is pretty unhelpful to be told that the undercarriage is not down as the plane lands; we really want to be assured that the program has been analysed to show that the situation will not arise.

This thought leads into the other problem with programming – ensuring that the implementation correctly implements the interface contract. This is often called debugging. Generally there are four ways in which bugs are found

(1) By the compiler. These are usually easy because the compiler tells us exactly what is wrong.

(2) At run time by a language check. This applies in languages which carry out checks that, for example, ensure that we do not write outside an array. Typically we obtain an error message saying what structure was violated and whereabouts in the program this happened.

(3) By testing. This means running various examples and poring over the (un)expected results and wondering where it all went wrong.

(4) By the program crashing. In olden days this resulted in a nice coredump which you could take home and browse over in the middle of the night. A similar modern effect is when Windows becomes remarkably silent because your application has written all over the operating system and usually destroyed the evidence. Reboot and try again!

Type 1 should really be extended to mean 'before the program is executed'. Thus it includes program walkthroughs and similar review techniques and, as we shall see, it includes the use of analysis tools such as those provided for SPARK. But many programs are just hacked together and the only static analysis they get is by the compiler.

Clearly these four ways provide a progression of difficulty. Errors are easier to locate and correct if they are detected early. Good programming tools are those which move bugs from one category to a lower numbered category. Thus good programming languages are those which provide facilities enabling one to protect oneself against errors that are hard to find. Strong typing is one example and the enumeration type is a simple feature which correctly used makes hard bugs of type 3 into easy bugs of type 1. This is discussed in more detail in Chapter 3.

Incidentally, it is sad to note that many popular and fashionable languages such as Java do not include proper enumeration types. The wave of enthusiasm for Object Orientation (OO) in all its dynamic glory (which indeed has its uses but by its very dynamic nature can create difficult problems) appears to have caused other established language features to be neglected with the consequence that many programmers no longer have the benefits of simple language-based debugging aids.

A major goal of SPARK is to enable the strengthening of interface definitions (the contracts) and so to move all errors to a low category and ideally to type 1 so that they are all found before the program executes. Thus the global annotations do this because they prevent us writing a program that accidentally changes the wrong global variables. Similarly, detecting the violation of pre- and postconditions in SPARK results in a type 1 error. However, in order to check that such violation cannot happen requires mathematical proof; this is not always straightforward but the SPARK tools automate much of the proof process as we shall see in Chapter 3.

1.3 Rationale for SPARK

As mentioned above the general goal of SPARK is to provide a language which increases the likelihood of the program behaving as intended. A corollary is to reduce to an acceptable level the risks of disaster arising as a result of any residual errors in the program.

The previous section outlined the benefits of strengthening interfaces (sometimes called programming by contract) but many other factors were also considered in the design of SPARK. The following paragraphs briefly discuss a number of these factors.

Logical soundness

For the behaviour of a program to be completely predictable, it is vital that the language in which it is written be precise. For example, most languages permit a statement such as

```
Y := F(X) + G(X);
```

but do not define the order of evaluation. As a consequence, if the functions F and G have side effects (by making assignments to X for example) then it is possible for the result assigned to Y to depend upon whether F or G is called first. This potential ambiguity does not arise in SPARK because functions cannot have side effects; functions are true mathematical functions which may observe the state of some part of the system but cannot change that state.

It is interesting to observe that the absence of ambiguity is achieved by preventing side effects and not by prescribing the order of the evaluations. In turn, the absence of side effects is not prescribed directly but, as we shall see, is a result of the interaction between a number of more fundamental rules.

Simplicity of language definition

Simplicity is generally considered to be good since it reduces the risk of a program actually meaning something different from what it appears to mean. Indeed, experience shows that parts of a language which cause complexity in any formal definition of the language are likely to be sources of problems.

Generally we can expect that simplicity of definition means simplicity of reasoning which implies simplicity of supporting tools and simplicity of testing. If tools are simpler then they are more likely to be reliable so that risks are reduced.

Expressive power

On the other hand, the language must not be so simple as to be trivial and not able to provide the key benefits of a modern language and its concepts of information hiding. Thus languages such as Basic, Pascal and C do not have enough expressive power largely because they do not have adequate facilities for hiding implementation details.

Another aspect is the need to be able to make stronger assertions about the values of variables and their relationships than is traditional in imperative programming languages. Such assertions clearly increase the expressive capability of the language.

Security and integrity

A language must be secure in the sense that it should not have rules that cannot be checked with reasonable effort (technically within polynomial time). Moreover the behaviour of any program must lie within certain well defined bounds. This is achieved by ensuring that the program does not stray outside a well defined computational model. In particular, a program must not be able to 'run wild' by jumping or writing to arbitrary locations.

Verifiability

Safety critical programs have to be shown to be correct. In order to do this it is necessary that the language constructions are such that a program can be subjected to rigorous mathematical analysis. For example it can be shown that goto statements impede analysis by making the decomposition of the flow of control intractable in the general case. It has been shown that it is highly desirable that every fragment of code has a single entry point and limited exit points. Thus the goto statement and arbitrary internal exits from loops and subprograms must be prevented.

It is also important to be able to analyse fragments of program on their own. This impacts on many aspects of the language such as the control of visibility.

Bounded space and time requirements

In order to prove that a program is able to function satisfactorily it is necessary to be able to predict the amount of storage space that it requires. So it must be possible to calculate the maximum amount of space required prior to execution, that is statically. General dynamic storage allocation is thus prohibited; in language terms this means that recursion, the declaration of arrays with dynamic bounds and especially pointer types and the use of heap storage have to be forbidden. It is interesting to note that recursion is not forbidden explicitly but cannot occur as a consequence of other rules in much the same way that side effects cannot occur as discussed above. The absence of recursion (direct and mutual) means that the depth of calls and hence the amount of stack space is bounded and can be computed statically.

Bounding time is more difficult. A real-time program that does not meet its deadlines is incorrect just as much as a numerical program that gives the wrong answer. SPARK is designed so that worst-case execution time analysis is possible if a manual analysis of loop bounds is carried out. At the time of writing, the Examiner does not implement this style of analysis. However, the Examiner does carry out some analysis of loops and gives warnings of certain non-terminating situations.

Correspondence with Ada

There are benefits in sharing technology and general resources with an existing standard language. However, these benefits can only be obtained if the special language truly is a subset of the parent language in the sense that compilers (and other tools) for the parent language can also be used for the special language. SPARK is indeed a true subset of Ada in this sense since any legal SPARK program is also a legal Ada program and, in addition, always executes with exactly the same meaning.

Note that SPARK does not impose additional requirements on the Ada compiler itself. Even though Ada permits an Ada program to mean different things using different implementations (that is, using different compilers) because of phenomena such as side effects, nevertheless the rules of SPARK are such that those Ada programs are not legal SPARK programs anyway.

Verifiability of compiled code

In an ideal world we would like to be assured that the compiled code does properly correspond to the source code written by the programmer. There would seem little point in carefully writing and verifying a program at the source level if bugs in the compiler mean that the object code does not exactly correspond to the source code. Thus we would like in turn to be assured that there are no bugs in the compiler. In principle it would seem easier to develop a correct compiler for a smaller language such as SPARK rather than for full Ada. However, such a compiler would be expensive to develop relative to the number of applications. There is also evidence that it is more reliable to use the well trodden parts of a widely used compiler for a larger language than to write and use a special compiler for an intrinsically simpler language.

Complexity of run time system

The final system delivered in an operational environment will typically comprise two parts, the code corresponding to that written by the programmer and a run time system written by the compiler developer which supports language features that cannot be sensibly implemented by inline code. The run time system is thus an integral part of the operational system and has to be shown to be correct (certified) just as much as the specific code for the application. Therefore the run time system must itself be capable of analysis.

Certifying a COTS (Commercial Off The Shelf) run time system for the most stringent standards such as DO-178B level A for commercial avionics systems [RTCA-EUROCAE, 1992] can be both arduous and very costly. The same applies to highly secure systems where many problems are blamed on the standard run time system of languages such as C [Wheeler, 2002].

SPARK has been designed so that it demands a very small run time system and, for some programs, none at all thereby avoiding at a stroke the costs and problems of certification.

It may not always be possible to avoid a run time system because, although most of the program can be written in a simple manner, nevertheless there may be some (less critical) parts that need more general facilities.

1.4   SPARK **language features**

The SPARK language comprises a kernel which is a subset of Ada plus additional features inserted as annotations in the form of Ada comments. These annotations are thus ignored by an Ada compiler and so a SPARK program can be compiled by a standard compiler.

The annotations are in two categories. The first category concerns flow analysis and visibility control and the second category concerns formal proof. The kernel plus the first category of annotations comprises the SPARK core language and the corresponding annotations are called the core annotations. The additional annotations concerning proof are referred to as the proof annotations. Thus SPARK comprises a core language plus optional features concerning proof. There is an interesting parallel with Ada which comprises a core language plus optional specialized annexes.

The relationship between SPARK and Ada is represented diagrammatically in Figure 1.1. This shows both languages comprising a core plus additional features. The overlap between them is the kernel. An important point is that SPARK should not be perceived as just a subset of Ada with a few bits tacked on in comments. SPARK should be seen as a language in its own right with just those facilities necessary for writing high integrity programs and permitting analysis and proof according to the needs of the application. For convenience SPARK and Ada overlap in terms of the compilable kernel for the very good reason of wishing to share compiler technology. Indeed it is clear that SPARK is not a subset of Ada at all since SPARK imposes additional requirements through the annotations.

(Incidentally, the term 'full Ada' is sometimes used for emphasis in the sense of 'as opposed to the kernel subset' and has nothing to do with the specialized annexes of Ada.)

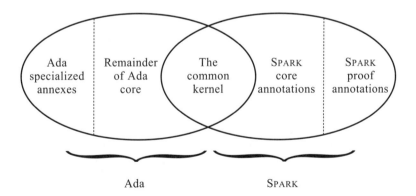

Figure 1.1   Relationship between SPARK and Ada.

Although the kernel language necessarily omits many features of full Ada it is nevertheless a rich language in its own right. It includes

- packages, private types, library units, type extension,
- unconstrained array types, functions returning composite types.

Thus SPARK contains a full capability for defining Abstract Data Types. Not only does it have private types giving information hiding but it also allows functions to return composite types. It also permits unconstrained array types as formal parameters so that subprograms can be written which will operate upon arrays of any size (although local arrays must have static size). SPARK also has facilities for separate compilation.

Note furthermore that SPARK includes type extension (a key feature of OO) but it does not include dynamic features such as polymorphism and dispatching since these cannot be proven statically; consequently it does not have class-wide types either.

At the time of writing SPARK does not include tasking facilities and indeed the full tasking capability of Ada would be impossible to analyse. However, it is planned that SPARK should support the so-called Ravenscar subset of Ada tasking in due course [Burns, Dobbing and Vardanega, 2003]. See Appendix 4.

The kernel also excludes the following features of full Ada

- exceptions, generics (templates),
- access (pointer) types, goto statements.

These are omitted largely on the grounds that they create difficulties in proving that a program is correct.

The core annotations take various forms. There are two important annotations regarding subprograms and these add further information to that provided by the specification in the Ada sense which simply gives the types and modes of the formal parameters.

- Global definitions – declare the use of global variables by subprograms.
- Dependency relations of procedures – specify the information flow between their imports and exports via both parameters and global variables.

These annotations should be seen as part of the specification of the contract between the subprogram and its callers and should be written at the design stage before coding is commenced. Of course, the information provided by these annotations just completes the static semantic description of the interface that the subprogram presents to the rest of the program. When the code of the subprogram body is written, the SPARK Examiner can be used to check that the code is consistent with the annotations.

On the other hand, once the code of the subprogram body is written, the annotations might be seen as simply providing an alternative view of information also existing in the implementation given in the subprogram body. This essential redundancy thereby gives confidence that the program is correct.

There is an analogy with hardware redundancy where physical replication of equipment gives confidence if the resulting measurements are consistent.

SPARK permits flow analysis at two levels: data flow analysis which just concerns the direction of data flow, and information flow analysis which also considers the coupling between variables. The dependency relation (familiarly known as the derives annotation) can be omitted if information flow analysis is not required but the global annotation is always necessary whenever global variables are used. Returning to our earlier example of the procedure Add, the specification including the derives annotation would be

```
procedure Add(X: in Integer);
--# global in out Total;
--# derives Total from Total, X;
```

In this particularly simple example, this actually adds no further information. We had already deduced that we had to use X and the initial value of Total in order to produce a new value of Total and this is precisely what this derives annotation says. But in more elaborate examples extra information is given. Thus we might have

```
procedure Add(X: in Integer);
--# global in out Total, Grand_Total;
--# derives Total from Total, X &
--#        Grand_Total from Grand_Total, X;
```

and now the derives annotation does provide additional information.

Other important core annotations concern access to variables in packages. Packages are the general means of encapsulation in SPARK. They provide the key facilities of Object Oriented Programming (OOP) by controlling access to hidden entities via subprograms (methods). The annotations relating to packages are

- Inherit clauses – control the visibility of package names.
- Own variable clauses – control access to package variables.
- Initialization annotations – indicate initialization of own variables.

Note that an *own* variable is one declared inside a package and which contains state preserved between calls of subprograms in the package. Own variables are an important feature of SPARK and can be used to represent abstractions encapsulating state of various forms. The initialization annotations ensure that it is impossible for such state not to be properly initialized and thereby prevent a variety of common programming errors. Own variables can also represent values in the physical world such as the readings of sensors and the settings of actuators.

A general guideline in the design of the fine detail of SPARK was to ensure that a SPARK program is as explicit as reasonably possible and that all potential ambiguities (whether in the mind of the compiler or the human reader) are eliminated wherever possible. This overall guideline is reflected in the following principles

- Overloading should be avoided as far as possible.
- Scope and visibility rules should be such that each entity has a unique name at a given place.
- All subtypes (types with constraints) should be named.
- All constraints (such as the size of arrays) should be static.
- Operations on complete arrays should be explicit wherever possible, implicit operations between arrays with different bounds (sliding) should be avoided.

The first three are closely related and concern the uniqueness of names. At any one place any entity should have only one name (no aliasing); each name should name only one entity (no overloading) and all entities should have a name (no anonymous entities). These principles are not followed exactly in every instance. For example, although the user cannot declare overloading of subprograms and enumeration literals, nevertheless the integer and floating point types inevitably have to use overloading for the predefined operations such as "+". However, the general observance of these principles does facilitate the rigorous analysis of SPARK programs and the uniqueness of names reduces the risk of confusion in the mind of the reader.

A number of further features of Ada are omitted on the grounds that they can also create confusion in the mind of the reader by introducing effects at a distance (that is the effect on the program is at a place remote from where the feature is used). These include such things as default parameters of subprograms.

Intrinsically unreliable features such as unchecked conversion (that is converting (casting) between values of unrelated types) are also prohibited in SPARK. However, where absolutely essential, they (and indeed any feature of full Ada) can be used in parts of a program covered by the special hide directive which tells the Examiner that a part of a program is not to be examined.

1.5   Tool support

The main SPARK tool, the Examiner, is vital to the use of SPARK. It has two basic functions

- It checks conformance of the code to the rules of the kernel language.
- It checks consistency between the code and the embedded annotations by control, data and information flow analysis.

The analysis performed by the SPARK Examiner is based largely on the analysis of the interfaces between components and ensuring that the details on either side do indeed conform to the specifications of the interfaces. The interfaces are of course the specifications of packages and subprograms and the

SPARK annotations say more about these interfaces and thereby improve the quality of the contract between the implementation of the component and its users.

The Examiner is itself written in SPARK and has been applied to itself. There is therefore considerable confidence in the correctness of the Examiner.

The SPARK language with its core annotations ensures that a program cannot have certain errors related to the flow of information. Thus the Examiner detects the use of uninitialized variables and the overwriting of values before they are used.

However, the core annotations do not address the issue of dynamic behaviour. In order to do this a number of proof annotations can be inserted such as the pre- and postconditions we saw earlier which enable dynamic behaviour to be analysed prior to execution. The general idea is that these annotations enable the Examiner to generate conjectures (potential theorems) which then have to be proved in order to verify that the program is correct with respect to the annotations. These proof annotations address

- pre- and postconditions of subprograms,
- assertions such as loop invariants and type assertions,
- declarations of proof functions and proof types.

The generated conjectures are known as verification conditions. These can then be verified by human reasoning, which is usually tedious and unreliable, or by using other tools such as the SPADE Automatic Simplifier (usually referred to as just the Simplifier) and the Proof Checker.

Even without proof annotations, the Examiner can generate conjectures corresponding to the run-time checks of Ada such as range checks. These are checks automatically inserted to ensure that a variable is not assigned a value outside the range permitted by its declaration or that no attempt is made to read or write outside the bounds of an array. The proof of these conjectures shows that the checks would not be violated and therefore that the program is free of run-time errors that would raise exceptions in full Ada.

It is important to understand that the use of proof is not necessary. SPARK and its tools can be used at various levels. For some applications it might be appropriate just to apply the core annotations because these alone enable flow analysis to be performed. Moreover, as already mentioned, flow analysis can be performed at two levels according to whether derives annotations are supplied or not. But for other applications it might be cost-effective to use the proof annotations as well. Indeed, different levels of analysis can be applied to different parts of a complete program. This is discussed in more detail in Chapter 3.

It should be noted that there are a number of advantages in using a distinct tool such as the Examiner rather than simply a front-end processor which then passes its output to a compiler. One general advantage is that it encourages the early use of a V & V (Verification and Validation) approach. Thus it is possible to write pieces of SPARK complete with annotations and to have them processed by the Examiner even before they can be compiled. For example, a package specification can be examined even though its private part might not yet be written; such an incomplete package specification cannot of course be compiled.

There is a temptation to take an existing piece of Ada code and then to add the annotations (often referred to as 'Sparking the Ada'). This is to be discouraged because it typically leads to extensive annotations indicative of an unnecessarily complex structure. Although in principle it might then be possible to rearrange the code to reduce the complexity, it is often the case that such good intentions are overridden by the desire to preserve as much as possible of the existing code.

The proper approach is to treat the annotations as part of the design process and to use them to assist in arriving at a design which minimizes complexity before the effort of detailed coding takes one down an irreversible path. This is discussed further in Chapter 12.

1.6 Examples

We conclude this introductory discussion with two further examples which illustrate a number of aspects of SPARK.

The first example leads on from that of the procedure Add which calculated a total and grand total by simulating the odometer of a vehicle. It records both the total distance travelled and the distance travelled on the current trip. The user can reset the trip recorder to zero but cannot change the setting of the total.

Each rotation of the wheel increments the counters by one and so a procedure Inc is provided for this rather than using Add. There are also functions for reading the current values of the counters.

The system is structured as a package encapsulating the subprograms and the counters. The specification of the package is

```
package Odometer
--# own Trip, Total: Integer;
is
   procedure Zero_Trip;
   --# global out Trip;
   --# derives Trip from ;
   --# post Trip = 0;

   function Read_Trip return Integer;
   --# global in Trip;

   function Read_Total return Integer;
   --# global in Total;

   procedure Inc;
   --# global in out Trip, Total;
   --# derives Trip from Trip & Total from Total;
   --# post Trip = Trip~ + 1 and Total = Total~ + 1;

end Odometer;
```

The important point of this example is to illustrate that the package specification provides just information regarding the interfaces and nothing else. It specifically contains no details of the workings of the implementation. But it is necessary to mention Trip and Total which are in fact hidden in the body in order to write the annotations and this is done using the own clause – later we shall see that own variables need not actually represent specific variables at all and so in fact we are not really giving away any information regarding the implementation.

A possible package body providing the implementation might be

```
package body Odometer is

   Trip, Total : Integer;

   procedure Zero_Trip is
   begin
      Trip := 0;
   end Zero_Trip;

   function Read_Trip return Integer is
   begin
      return Trip;
   end Read_Trip;

   function Read_Total return Integer is
   begin
      return Total;
   end Read_Total;

   procedure Inc is
   begin
      Trip := Trip + 1;  Total := Total + 1;
   end Inc;

end Odometer;
```

It is interesting to observe that there are no annotations in the body. This emphasizes the point that SPARK is largely about increasing the information regarding interface specifications. We have omitted a number of minor details such as how the variable Total becomes initialized and what happens if the counters overflow. In fact the Examiner warns us about the initialization of Total – we shall return to this example in Section 13.2.

But the key point of the example is to show how well the separation of interface specification from implementation body provided perhaps uniquely by Ada suits the goals of SPARK. Even modern languages such as Java confuse the issues by presenting the two aspects as a single lump of text. For those not familiar with Ada the example also illustrates the general style of the language which hopefully should be self-explanatory.

The second example illustrates how SPARK can detect possible errors in small-scale aspects of programming. In order to appreciate the example it must be pointed out that array parameters in Ada can be passed by reference or by copy. Thus a compiler might choose to pass large arrays by reference and small arrays by copy. Consider the following procedure to multiply two matrices X and Y giving the result in Z.

```
type Matrix_Index is range 0 .. 9;
type Matrix is array (Matrix_Index, Matrix_Index) of Integer;
...

procedure Multiply(X, Y: in Matrix; Z: out Matrix)
--# derives Z from X, Y;
is
begin
   Z := Matrix'(Matrix_Index => (Matrix_Index => 0));   -- zero Z
   for I in Matrix_Index loop
      for J in Matrix_Index loop
         for K in Matrix_Index loop
            Z(I, J) := Z(I, J) + X(I, K) * Y(K, J);
         end loop;
      end loop;
   end loop;
end Multiply;
```

The type declarations indicate that objects of the type Matrix_Index are integers and can only have values in the range 0 to 9 and that arrays of the type Matrix have two dimensions and are indexed in both dimensions by values of the type Matrix_Index. Accordingly all arrays of the type Matrix have 100 components. Finally these components have values of the predefined type Integer.

The procedure Multiply takes the two arrays passed as the parameters X and Y and multiplies them together in the normal mathematical manner to produce the array Z. However, the procedure call

```
Multiply(A, A, A);
```

intended to replace a matrix A by its square will instead nullify A if the arrays are passed by reference rather than by copy. However, in SPARK this procedure call is illegal because it violates the rules about aliasing – an actual parameter cannot correspond to both an imported parameter (such as X) and an exported parameter (such as Z).

When the Examiner examines the call of Multiply it reports

```
***        Semantic Error:165: This parameter is overlapped
           by another one which is exported.
```

for the first two parameters and so the program is rejected. (The number 165 is the error reference number and enables the user to read more details regarding the cause of the error in the user manual.) Note that the Examiner detects such aliasing errors whatever level of flow analysis is used.

It is interesting to note that SPARK does not require parameter passing to be by reference or by copy, it just imposes other restrictions that ensure that they give the same result so that it does not matter. (Just imposing a restriction on the parameter mechanism itself would actually violate the goal of the SPARK kernel being a subset of Ada because it would mean that a particular program well-defined in SPARK might have a different meaning in Ada.)

We conclude by emphasizing once more that the global and derives annotations are part of the procedure specification. As we have seen, it is usual for the specification and body to be distinct – this is always so for packages but it is not always necessary for procedures and by way of illustration we have shown the two combined in this example. In the case of distinct specification and body, the annotations are not repeated in the body; if there is no distinct specification then they occur in the body before the reserved word **is** as shown here. The annotations separate the interaction between the caller and the specification from that between the specification and the implementation, just as the Ada parameter profile specifies enough for the subprogram to be called without regard to the details of the body. Hence the Examiner carries out two sets of checks: it checks that the annotations are consistent with the procedure body (which they are) and it also checks that the annotations are consistent with all calls (which is not so for the call in this example).

Other points to be noted from this example are that in SPARK the bounds of arrays have to be given by a name (Index_Range in this case) and that the bounds have to be static. Note also the assignment to Z in order to set all components of Z to zero; the construction is known as a qualified aggregate and takes a nested form since Z has two dimensions. The reader might wonder why we did not use a nested loop – the reason is that this would cause certain problems with flow analysis as will be discussed in Section 6.7.

1.7   Historical note

SPARK has its technical origins in work carried out in the 1970s at the then Royal Signals and Radar Establishment (RSRE) by the late Bob Phillips. (RSRE at Great Malvern in the UK is now part of the QinetiQ (*sic*) Group plc.) Phillips was interested in understanding and analysing the behaviour of existing programs and developed tools to perform such analysis. However, it was soon realized that analysis would be easier if the programs were written in a sensible language in the first place. There was also growing awareness of the importance of the correctness of software for safety critical applications such as the control of aircraft.

A group at Southampton University led by Bernard Carré doing research in the field of graph theory then became closely involved; the group developed tools for a subset of Pascal called SPADE – or more grandly the Southampton Program Analysis Development Environment. It was of course realized that Pascal was an inadequate base because it did not address separate compilation and information hiding. An alternative foundation language was hence sought.

There were two obvious possibilities at the time, Modula-2 (whose industrial future was already in doubt) and Ada. The C language was dismissed on the grounds of the lack of an international standard and its general permissiveness. Ada on the other hand was an international standard, was strongly supported among those application areas interested in high integrity software, included packages for encapsulation and moreover had a lexical distinction between the specification and body of a package which was important for the description of interface contracts. It was also eminently readable with clean syntax amenable to both human and machine analysis.

Accordingly, Ada was chosen as the foundation for future work. It was of course necessary to exclude certain features of Ada from programs that were to be analysed by the SPADE tools and this resulted in the SPADE Ada Kernel or SPARK. However, as we have seen, SPARK is not just a subset of Ada but also requires embedded annotations giving extra information about the program; these annotations take the form of Ada comments so that the program is still strictly an Ada program.

SPARK was originally defined informally by Bernard Carré and Trevor Jennings of Southampton University in 1988. This Specification described SPARK as a variation on Ada using the usual syntax together with informal semantics. It was subsequently defined formally using a variant of Z in *The Formal Semantics of SPARK* which comprises two main parts addressing the static and dynamic semantics respectively [Marsh and O'Neill, 1994].

In 1995, the Ada standard itself was revised resulting in Ada 95. Although most of the changes to Ada were outside the subset on which SPARK was based, nevertheless some changes to Ada were quite fundamental and very relevant to SPARK. The opportunity was thus taken to upgrade SPARK and the resulting language was defined in a new version of the Specification by Gavin Finnie. SPARK has evolved further since then and the version current at the time of writing is [Praxis, 2002]; it is this version, based on Ada 95, which forms the subject of this book. Whenever it is necessary to distinguish the old and new versions they are referred to as SPARK 83 and SPARK 95 respectively.

Those familiar with the evolution of Ada 83 into Ada 95 will note that many of the facilities added in Ada 95 are not available in SPARK. This is almost inevitable because most of the new facilities in Ada 95 were added in order to increase dynamic flexibility – that is to give more flexibility at run time. But this is precisely what SPARK is not about; in order to prove that a program is correct, it is necessary that dynamic flexibility be kept to a minimum. However, a number of changes to Ada which were made to ease the static burden on the programmer have also been made to SPARK. The most obvious of these are the introduction of child packages and type extension. Other changes include the introduction of the use type clause, the ability to read out parameters, the clarification of the rules for conformance, and the removal of the petty restriction on the order of declarations. Perhaps surprisingly, the ability to read out parameters had far reaching effects; it permitted the introduction of global annotations with mode information and this in turn allowed greater flexibility in flow analysis by enabling it to be performed at two different levels.

A recent publication in the standards area is the *Guide for the Use of the Ada Programming Language in High Integrity Systems* [ISO, 2000]. This contains excellent general background material on the whole topic and in particular gives guidance on which features of Ada are appropriate for use with various verification techniques.

1.8   Structure of this book

The purpose of this book is to provide an overall description of the use of SPARK for writing reliable software. It is intended that knowledge of Ada is not required since all features are described in reasonable detail. In those cases where all the details are not given (such as interfacing to hardware using address clauses) it is inevitable that the user will have to refer to the compiler vendor's literature anyway.

However, since it is expected that some readers will have a working knowledge of Ada, various comparative remarks have been included which it is hoped will be helpful. These are largely confined to the ends of sections so that they do not impede the general reader. Those wishing to know more about Ada could consult *Programming in Ada 95* by the author [Barnes, 1998]. The ultimate reference for Ada is of course the *Ada Reference Manual* [Taft et al., 2000]; this is usually referred to as the *ARM*.

The description of SPARK as a language is (intended to be) complete apart from a few features such as fixed point arithmetic. However, the discussion of the use of the SPARK tools for proof is simply an introduction. There are many matters of detail which are not included partly because they would occupy a great deal of space and also because they are best learnt through practical interactive tuition and experience. Thus only the general principles of proof are described and the interactive use of the Proof Checker is barely covered.

The CD accompanying this book contains additional documentation as well as demonstration versions of the Examiner and Simplifier plus all necessary installation information and user guides. The Proof Checker is not included on the CD but is available with professional versions of the other tools from Praxis Critical Systems.

This book is in three main parts. The first part, Chapters 1 to 3, is an overview of the topic and introduces the reader to most of the features of SPARK and its associated tools in an informal manner and illustrates the language and the tools with some small examples.

The second part, Chapters 4 to 8, comprises a thorough description of the SPARK core language. The syntax notation is widely used because it enables a precise description to be given in a compact and clear manner. It is anticipated that this part of the book will be found most useful as reference material.

The third part, Chapters 9 to 14, covers in more detail the use of the various associated tools and also describes their theoretical background. It is written in a more tutorial style and contains many examples including some case studies of complete programs.

The book concludes with a number of appendices covering such matters as the complete syntax and lists of reserved words and attributes.

Most chapters have a few exercises; the reader should at least attempt these and consult the answers because they cover a number of quite notable points and are sometimes referred to in later material. The CD contains the text of all the major examples and exercises and the reader might find it instructive to apply the Examiner and (where appropriate) the Simplifier to them. Further details will be found in Appendix 3.

The final chapter of the book is Chapter 14 entitled Case Studies. This has three examples, one is a lift controller, the second is an autopilot and the third concerns the proof of a sorting algorithm. The chapter concludes with a summary of some industrial applications which is reproduced below.

This sampler itself concludes with the bibliography which contains a number of useful website references.

14.9   Industrial applications

The subtitle of this book is 'The SPARK Approach to Safety and Security' and so it is fitting to conclude by outlining a number of projects which have used SPARK in both the Safety and Security areas. As mentioned in Section 1.1, a key aspect to providing safe and secure systems that involve software is getting the software correct. It is of no avail if hardware backup systems are in place or clever cryptography is used if the actual code is wrong.

Moreover, SPARK not only helps to get the code correct but it also provides concrete auditable evidence that it is correct in the form of POGS output and analysis logs. This is vital for the certification of high integrity systems.

The value of SPARK in getting the code correct has long been recognized for military systems and so SPARK can be considered to be tried and trusted technology even if it may not be familiar to the reader. Moreover, since around 1990, its use has spread and it is now used on many large-scale industrial projects mainly in the aerospace, rail and security areas.

Three notable projects are briefly described below in order to give the reader some appreciation of the importance and scale of typical applications. Two are from the safety critical area and one is from the security area.

These three projects also illustrate the SPARK approach to three very different software standards: DO-178B for civil aviation, ITSEC (Information Technology Security Evaluation Criteria) and more recently the Common Criteria [ISO, 1999] for secure systems, and Def-Stan 00-55 for military safety-related software.

The first project uses DO-178B and the project description is followed by a brief discussion of data and control coupling as defined by DO-178B and how SPARK is perhaps uniquely able to satisfy these aspects of its objectives.

The Lockheed Martin C130J and DO-178B

The C130J is a remarkable aircraft. It shares the familiar Hercules airframe with its predecessors, but features entirely new engines, propellers and avionics. The Mission Computer is a DO-178B Level A system that controls most of the aircraft's major functions. It comprises over 100,000 lines of code, most of which is written in SPARK.

DO-178B is an interesting standard. It places great emphasis on particular forms of testing, but has little to say on issues such as choice of programming language or the use of static analysis. Testing such software can be time-consuming and expensive so that if defects are found during testing, the rework implied significantly increases both the cost and timescale of the process.

An alternative, therefore, is simply not to rely on testing as the only verification activity. The cheapest way to run a DO-178B testing process is to just write the software correctly in the first place.

This is of course the SPARK approach – the static analysis offered by the Examiner and Simplifier eliminate so many defects that the testing process becomes cheaper, simpler and (ideally) a one-off demonstration of correctness rather than being a repetitive bug-hunt. The use of run-time check (RTC) proof also means that you can *justifiably* turn off run-time checks in your code, which dramatically simplifies the generated object code and subsequent coverage analysis.

Perceived productivity is an important issue. Many program managers (and tool vendors) equate productivity in software engineering with the number of lines of code produced per day. Such statistics are misleading. Coding usually accounts for a small proportion of a total project (typically 10–20%) while testing, integration and certification are typically over 50%, and can be as high as 80% in some cases. Slowing down coding a little to ease testing a great deal makes sound economic sense. On the C130J, the use of SPARK certainly *slowed* coding, but led to such a dramatic improvement in testing that significant costs were saved as a result.

Of course the use of SPARK was but one technology involved. Much credit must also be given to the maturity of the life cycle processes used and the way in which they integrated together. Nevertheless it is recognized that SPARK made a major contribution. Eventually, after all the numbers were added up and accounted for, Lockheed reported an 80% saving over their projected cost for testing and certification of the Mission Computer [Amey, 2002].

Data and control coupling and DO-178B

The SPARK approach is a sound technique for producing high integrity software of various kinds. The previous example discussed the use of DO-178B for a particular application. DO-178B has many objectives that must be satisfied, but does not require the use of an approach similar to SPARK to satisfy its requirements. One objective, however, is particularly troublesome, and SPARK presents an approach which can be used to provide evidence which is hard to obtain using other techniques.

DO-178B requires the analysis of data and control coupling for Levels A, B and C software. It defines data and control coupling as follows

Data coupling – the dependence of a software component on data not exclusively under the control of that software component.

Control coupling – the manner or degree by which one software component influences the execution of another software component.

DO-178B does not provide a basis for why analysis of data and control coupling is required nor does it explain how it should be achieved. The purpose of data and control coupling analysis is to serve as a 'goodness' or completion check of the integration effort. Analysis of data and control coupling is intended to ensure good software engineering practices.

The software components may be packages or subprograms. DO-178B has many objectives which together provide evidence that each of the software components satisfies its requirements. Some of these components will be grouped because they share global data, and some because they are interrelated through some control logic. When these components are integrated, there is a need to show that information flows in a controlled manner as expected by the design. By using SPARK annotations to describe the expected information flow between software components, the design can express the data coupling between software components, even when they are separately compiled. The SPARK tools can be used to verify the coupling expected by design against the coupling provided by the source code itself.

The SPARK approach enables engineers to describe the dependency of one component on another in terms of the data and control they share. The verification of this dependency against the code, before the code is linked, eliminates possible integration problems between the software components. The evidence that this has been done can be used to help satisfy the requirements for the verification of data and control coupling.

The MULTOS CA and secure systems

The MULTi-application Operating System (MULTOS) is a smartcard OS that allows several applications to reside on a single card. MULTOS applications can be loaded and deleted dynamically, so a major security concern is the prevention of forged applications. To this end, a MULTOS application is accompanied by a digital certificate that is signed by the MULTOS Certification Authority (CA).

The CA was built as far as was practicable to meet the highest standard of the UK ITSEC scheme. SPARK therefore seemed appropriate for the most security critical aspects of the system. However, SPARK was obviously not appropriate for all parts of the system and so a 'right tools for the job' mix of languages was used. The whole system is about 100,000 lines of code, about 30% of which is in SPARK for the most security critical functions, about 30% is in Ada 95, mainly in the system infrastructure, and 30% is in C++, for the graphical user interface (GUI). The remaining 10% is in a mixture of C (for some standard cryptographic algorithms) and SQL. Note that the system was very carefully designed so that the GUI does not have any security-related function.

The static analysis offered by SPARK proved to be most effective. Data flow errors can cause subtle security problems – for example, an uninitialized variable might just acquire an initial value which happens to be a piece of cryptographic key material 'left over' on the stack from the execution of another subprogram. Knowing that the use of SPARK prevented such problems was important.

Information flow analysis also proved useful. The separation of some data sections (so that information in variable X cannot leak into variable Y) gave confidence that certain security properties were being maintained by the code.

RTC proof also offered strong protection against the ubiquitous buffer overflow problems that seem to plague software written in weaker languages.

The MULTOS CA demonstrates the use of SPARK in a large, mixed-language development. The system has been extremely reliable since it was commissioned; in the first year after delivery, four minor defects were reported – a rate of 0.04 defects per thousand lines of code. The project was also completed at reasonable cost (some 3571 person days) and productivity (28 lines of code per day for the entire project).

This experience belies the myth that a project implemented to such a high standard must be prohibitively expensive. Further details on how the CA was constructed can be found in [Hall and Chapman, 2002].

SHOLIS and Def-Stan 00-55

The Ship/Helicopter Operational Limits Instrumentation System (SHOLIS) is a ship-borne computer system that advises ship's crew on the safety of helicopter operations under various scenarios. It is a fault-tolerant, real-time, embedded system. A pre-production version of SHOLIS was originally developed during 1996 to 1998 and was the first system aimed to meet all the requirements of UK Interim Defence Standard 00-55 for safety critical software.

Def Stan 00-55 places great emphasis on the use of rigorous notations and processes, and actually requires the use of static analysis and programming languages that have an 'unambiguous definition'. As such, SPARK remains the only language that can seriously claim to meet this standard.

SHOLIS was the first major effort to use the SPARK proof technology on an industrial scale. (SHOLIS is about 27,000 lines of code, so it is not a toy program by any means.) SHOLIS also extended the scope of any proof work that had ever been attempted previously; RTC proof was performed on the entire system, while safety critical subsystems were also subject to proofs of partial correctness and safety properties that were derived from the formal specification of the system. While this might seem like a great deal of work, subsequent analysis of the project showed that the specification and code proof were extremely cost-effective at preventing and finding defects – certainly much more effective than the subsequent unit-testing process [King et al., 2000].

In 1996, machine resources were a limiting factor – it really was not possible to get enough computing power for the Simplifier. Today, all the SHOLIS proofs (some 9000 verification conditions) can be generated and simplified in about eight hours on a modest desktop computer thereby bringing 'regression proof' into scope for industrial scale applications.

In conclusion

It is hoped that these three industrial examples have illustrated that SPARK is a professional product in real use for serious programs that need to be correct. Experience has shown that, in conjunction with good project management, the use of SPARK both saves money and increases the predictability of project timescales and moreover, by eliminating residual errors, reduces long-term maintenance costs.

Bibliography

The following items are referred to in the body of the text.

[Amey, 2002]   Peter Amey, Correctness by Construction: Better can also be Cheaper, *CrossTalk Journal*, pp. 24–28, March 2002. {www.stsc.hill.af.mil and www.sparkada.com}

[Barnes, 1998]   J. G. P. Barnes, *Programming in Ada 95*, 2nd edn, Addison-Wesley, Harlow, 1998, ISBN 0-201-34293-6.

[Bergeretti and Carré, 1985]   J.-F. Bergeretti and B. A. Carré, Information-Flow and Data-Flow Analysis of while-Programs, *ACM Transactions on Programming Languages and Systems*, ACM, New York, Vol. 7, pp. 37–61, Jan. 1985.

[Böhm and Jacopini, 1966]   C. Böhm and G. Jacopini, Flow Diagrams, Turing Machines, and Languages with Only Two Formation Rules, *Communications of the ACM*, ACM, New York, Vol. 19, no. 5, May 1966.

[Burns, Dobbing and Vardanega, 2003]   A. Burns, B. J. Dobbing and T. Vardanega, *Guide for the Use of the Ada Ravenscar Profile in High Integrity Systems*, University of York Technical Report YCS-2003-348, 2003. {ftp.cs.york.ac.uk/reports/YCS-2003-348.pdf}

[Farrow, Kennedy and Zucconi, 1975]   R. Farrow, K. Kennedy and L. Zucconi, Graph Grammars and Global Program Flow Analysis, *Proceedings of 17th IEEE Symposium on Foundations of Computer Science*, pp. 42–56, IEEE, New York, 1975.

[Hall and Chapman, 2002]   Anthony Hall and Roderick Chapman, Correctness by Construction: Building a commercial secure system, *IEEE Software*, Vol. 19, no. 1, pp. 18–25, Jan./Feb. 2002. {www.sparkada.com}

[ISO, 1999]   International Standards Organization, *Common Criteria for Information Technology Security Evaluation*, ISO/IEC 15408:1999.

[ISO, 2000]   International Standards Organization, *Guide for the Use of the Ada Programming Language in High Integrity Systems*, ISO/IEC TR 15942: 2000.

[King et al., 2000]   Steve King, Jonathan Hammond, Roderick Chapman and Andy Prior, Is Proof More Cost-Effective Than Testing?, *IEEE Transactions on Software Engineering*, Vol. 26, no. 8, pp. 675–686, August 2000. {www.sparkada.com}

[Marsh and O'Neill, 1994]   D. W. R. Marsh and I. M. O'Neill, *The Formal Semantics of SPARK*, Program Validation Ltd, Southampton, 1994. {www.sparkada.com}

[Meyer, 1992]   Bertrand Meyer, *Eiffel: The Language*, Prentice Hall, 1992, ISBN 0-132-47925-7.

[Praxis, 2002]   *SPARK 95 – The SPADE Ada Kernel*, Edition 3.1, Praxis Critical Systems Limited, October 2002.

[RTCA-EUROCAE, 1992]   *Software Considerations in Airborne Systems and Equipment Certification*, DO-178B/ED-12B, RTCA-EUROCAE, December 1992.

[SPC, 1995]   The Software Productivity Consortium, *Ada 95 Quality and Style*, LNCS 1344, Springer-Verlag, Berlin, 1995, ISBN 3-540-63823-7.

[Taft et al., 2000]   S. Tucker Taft, Robert A. Duff, Randall L. Bruckardt and Erhard Ploedereder (eds.), *Consolidated Ada Reference Manual*, LNCS 2219, Springer-Verlag, Berlin, 2000, ISBN 3-540-43038-5.

[Warshall, 1962]   S. Warshall, A Theorem on Boolean Matrices, *Journal of the ACM*, Vol. 9, pp. 11–13, Jan. 1962.

[Wheeler, 2002]   David A. Wheeler, *Secure Programming for Linux and Unix HOWTO*, 2002. {www.dwheeler.com/secure-programs/Secure-Programs-HOWTO/index.html}

The following papers give additional information on SPARK and its tools. Most will be found on the website www.sparkada.com.

P. Amey, Logic versus Magic in Critical Systems, *Reliable Software Technologies – Ada-Europe 2001*, LNCS 2043, Springer-Verlag, Berlin, 2001.

> This paper was given as a keynote address at Ada-Europe 2001. It presents SPARK as an example of a logical approach to engineering in contrast to the non-mathematical wizardry of other approaches. It also includes an interesting comparison between the current state of software engineering and the early days of aerodynamics.

P. Amey, Closing the Loop: The influence of code analysis on design, *Reliable Software Technologies – Ada-Europe 2002*, LNCS 2361, Springer-Verlag, Berlin, 2002.

> This paper discusses how the need to perform static analysis has a profound impact on the design of software. Based on the experience of several projects, some using SPARK and INFORMED and some not, it argues that the ability to statically analyse a software design at all

stages in its development should be a primary design goal in the
development of high integrity systems.

P. Amey, A Language for Systems not just Software, *Proceedings of SIGAda
2001*, ACM, New York, 2001.

> This paper demonstrates how SPARK's support for abstraction and
> refinement can be used to specify system-level properties of a software
> artefact. This enables the annotations to be in terms of concrete
> devices such as sensors and actuators so that they can be constructed
> and meaningfully checked by systems engineers.

P. Amey and R. Chapman, Industrial Strength Exception Freedom,
Proceedings of SIGAda 2002, ACM, New York, 2002.

> This paper describes the SPARK approach to eliminating exceptions
> arising from run-time checks as described in Chapter 11 of this book.
> It gives results for several large programs, including the Examiner
> itself; these show the effectiveness of the Simplifier in proving VCs
> and the performance of the Simplifier on modest PC hardware. The
> paper argues that the routine use of such proof is now within the reach
> of all SPARK projects.

R. Chapman, SPARK – A State-of-the-Practice Approach to the Common
Criteria Implementation Requirements, *2nd International Common
Criteria Conference*, Brighton UK, July 2001.

> This paper shows how SPARK meets the Common Criteria requirements
> for the implementation of secure systems. In particular, the Common
> Criteria require the use of notations that have an 'unambiguous
> definition' – an area where SPARK clearly excels. The paper also
> illustrates how SPARK and the Examiner can be used to defend software
> against many common forms of security vulnerability such as dataflow
> errors and the ubiquitous buffer overflow.

R. Chapman and A. Burns, Combining Static Worst-Case Timing Analysis and
Program Proof, *Real-Time Systems*, Vol. 11, pp. 145–171, 1996.

> This paper is a condensed form of the first author's doctoral thesis. It
> shows how the SPARK model of control flow and proof can be extended
> to deal with worst-case static analysis of time and memory usage. It
> also proposes additional annotations to enable subprograms to declare
> their required computation time, loop iteration bounds and so on.

R. Chapman and R. Dewar, Re-engineering a Safety-Critical Application Using
SPARK 95 and GNORT, *Reliable Software Technologies – Ada-Europe '99*,
LNCS 1622, Springer-Verlag, Berlin, 1999.

> This paper reports on an experiment to port the SHOLIS (SPARK 83)
> software to SPARK 95 using the GNAT Pro High Integrity Edition
> compiler. This demonstrated (some ten years after the original design

decision was made) that SPARK really could be compiled with a 'zero byte run time system'.

M. Croxford and J. M. Sutton, Breaking Through the V & V Bottleneck, *Ada in Europe 1995*, LNCS 1031, Springer-Verlag, Berlin, 1995.

This paper presents a method of software development aimed at 'correctness by construction', which greatly attenuates problems and costs associated with the detection of errors at a late phase of the lifecycle. The process described here has been applied to the development of avionic software for the C-130J aircraft.

The following books provide more general background reading.

R. C. Backhouse, *Program Construction and Verification*, Prentice-Hall International, Englewood Cliffs, New Jersey, 1986.

D. Gries, *The Science of Programming*, Springer-Verlag, Berlin, 1981.

S. S. Muchnik and N. D. Jones (eds), *Program Flow Analysis*, Prentice-Hall International, Englewood Cliffs, New Jersey, 1981.

C. T. Sennett (ed.), *High-integrity Software*, Pitman, London, 1989.

J. Woodcock and M. Loomes, *Software Engineering Mathematics*, Pitman, London, 1988; and Addison-Wesley, Reading, Massachussetts, 1989.